CW00541570

DIDCOT TO SWINDON

Vic Mitchell and Keith Smith

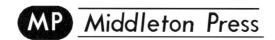

MP Middleton Press

Cover picture: Swindon was considered by many to be the centre of the GWR and a small group of railway observers enjoy its unique ambience on 4th April 1946, while a local train waits to leave from the long-lost down platform. (H.C.Casserley)

Published July 2002

ISBN 1 901706 84 2

© Middleton Press, 2002

Design   Deborah Esher
Typesetting   Barbara Mitchell

Published by
           Middleton Press
           Easebourne Lane
           Midhurst, West Sussex
           GU29 9AZ
Tel: 01730 813169
Fax: 01730 812601

Printed & bound by Biddles Ltd,
           Guildford and Kings Lynn

INDEX

ACKNOWLEDGEMENTS

We are very grateful for the help received from many of the photographers mentioned in the credits and also for the assistance given by T. Bryan, W.R.Burton, R.S.Carpenter, G.Croughton, M.Dart, G.Heathcliffe, M.King, N.Langridge, B.W.Leslie, Mr D. & Dr. S.Salter, T.Smith, N.W.Sprinks, G.T.V.Stacey, E.Youldon and our ever helpful wives, Barbara Mitchell and Janet Smith.

I. Railway Clearing House map from 1947.

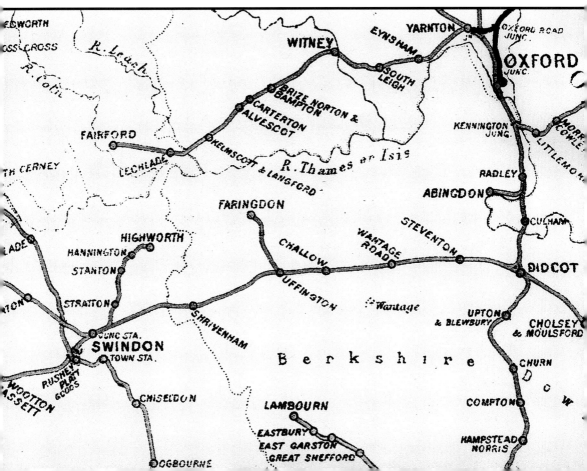

GEOGRAPHICAL SETTING

The entire route runs parallel to the scarp edge of the Berkshire Downs. These are formed of Chalk under which are strata of Upper Greensand and Gault Clay. It is on these that most of the track was laid. Into the Chalk was cut the shape of a horse, this giving rise to the name of the Vale of the White Horse for the area.

Only one watercourse of note is crossed, that being the small River Cole one mile west of Shrivenham, which marked the Berkshire/Wiltshire boundary, until recently.

The 25 mile long route rises from about 200 to 300ft above sea level from Didcot to Swindon. The branch to Highworth climbs near its terminus to almost 400ft, as the town is situated on a ridge of Corallian Limestone.

The maps are at the scale of 25ins to 1 mile, unless indicated otherwise. North is at the top, except where there is an arrow.

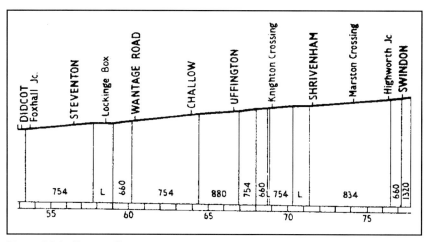

II.   Main line gradient

III.   Faringdon branch   IV.   Highworth branch

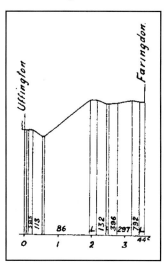

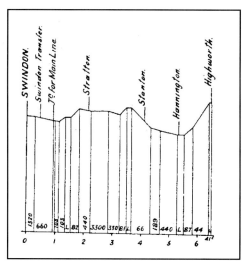

HISTORICAL BACKGROUND

The Great Western Railway reached Reading from London in March 1840. The engineer was I.K.Brunel and it was constructed under an Act of Parliament dated 31st August 1835.

The line was extended beyond Reading to Didcot and on to Steventon on 1st June 1840, the entire route being built to the broad gauge of 7ft 0¼ins. The section to Faringdon Road (later Challow) opened on 20th July 1840 and the link to Hay Lane (three miles beyond Swindon) followed on 17th December 1840. Trains reached Bristol on 30th June 1841 and a branch from Didcot to Oxford opened on 12th June 1844. The route received third rails in February 1872 and the broad gauge was finally abolished on 21st May 1892.

The associated branches opened and closed to public passenger service thus:

	Opened (passengers)	Closed (passengers)	Closed (goods)
Wantage Road to Wantage	11-10-1875	1-8-1925	19-12-1945
Uffington to Faringdon	1-6-1864	31-12-1951	1-7-1963
Swindon to Highworth	9-5-1883	2-3-1953	6-8-1962
Swindon to Cirencester	31-5-1841	Open to Gloucester	

There were no major changes when the GWR was nationalised in 1948, to become the Western Region of British Railways. Trains began to appear in sector liveries - InterCity and Network SouthEast - in the mid-1980s - these being followed in the mid-1990s by Thames Trains and Great Western Trains colours as a prelude to privatisation. The former franchise was let on 13th October 1996 and the latter on 4th February of the same year; the owning companies became Victory Railway Holdings and First Group respectively. Virgin Cross Country trains and Thames Trains only appear at Didcot, trains on the remainder of the route being branded First Great Western, with the exception of one nocturnal service operated on the route by Wales & Borders Trains. However, the Oxford-Bristol FGW operation was sub-contracted to Thames Trains.

PASSENGER SERVICES

We consider in this section down trains running at least five days per week and in the first table fast trains are non-stop or one stop and the slows called at most stations. Stopping trains were withdrawn completely on 7th December 1964 and no trace of buildings remain at the intermediate stations.

	Weekdays		Sundays	
	Fast	Slow	Fast	Slow
1848	3	8	-	-
1869	4	6	1	3
1889	6	6	1	3
1909	8	7	1	1
1929	8	6	7	2
1949	8	9	7	3
1964	16	4	10	-
1999	44	-	35	-

Faringdon branch

For the first few weeks there were only four weekday trains. The last Sunday services operated in 1875, but one or two milk trains continued to run on Sundays until closure.

	Weekdays	Sundays
1865	6	3
1870	7	4
1889	5	-
1909	12	-
1929	10	-
1934	4	-
1951	6	-

Highworth branch

The up train frequency is shown in this table.

	Weekdays	Sundays
1883	5	-
1909	6	2
1930	4	2
1952	3	-

There was one Sunday train in 1899-1906 and two in 1908-32.

1909

1951

1909

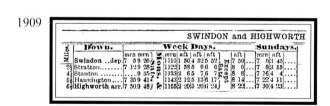

1952

DIDCOT PARKWAY

V.   The 1883 survey at 6ins to 1 mile includes the village of under 400 souls and its contemporary spelling, which was never used by the railway. The station opened on 12th June 1844 with the branch to Oxford (top) and four years after the main line. The "Loop Line" was brought into use on 22nd December 1856 as a means of speeding trains on the route to the Midlands, which was completed in 1852.

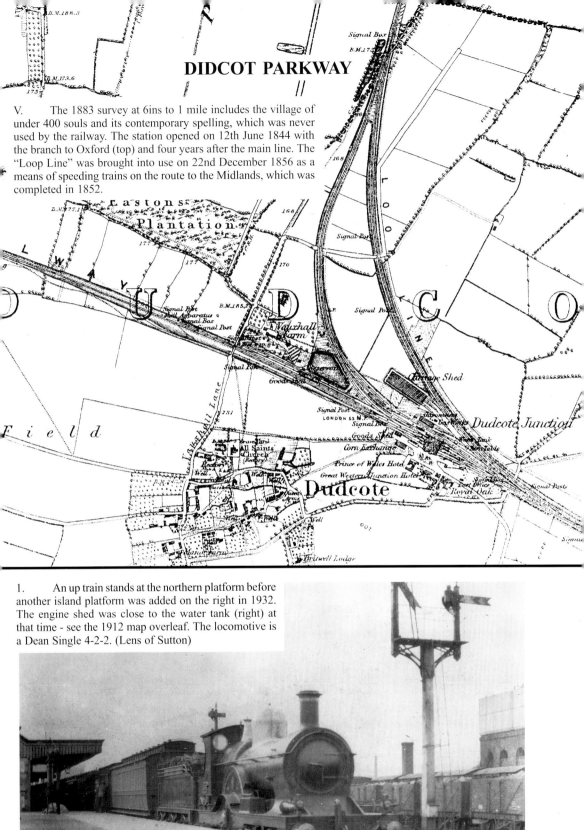

1.   An up train stands at the northern platform before another island platform was added on the right in 1932. The engine shed was close to the water tank (right) at that time - see the 1912 map overleaf. The locomotive is a Dean Single 4-2-2. (Lens of Sutton)

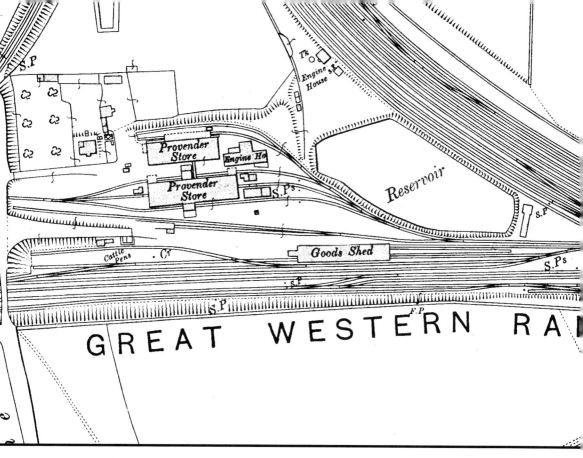

VI.   In the top left corner of this 1912 map is part of West Curve, which opened on 15th February 1886. The station had four through lines and an overall roof until it was rebuilt as shown in about 1884.

2.   The west end of the station was recorded in 1919, the area being known as "Chester Line Junction". Chester was the northern limit of the GWR for many years. West End signal box was replaced in 1932 by one to the north of the new quadruple track. (LGRP/NRM)

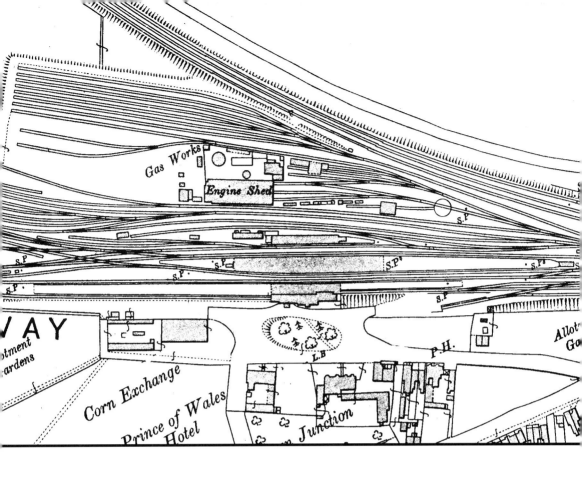

Gas Works

Engine Shed

Corn Exchange

Prince of Wales Hotel

Junction

Allotment Gardens

P.H.

L.B.

3.   The new island platform is on the left of this 1932 photograph, which was taken from a point near the centre of the previous picture after the old island platform had been lengthened. Note that part of the canopy remained curved. (LGRP/NRM)

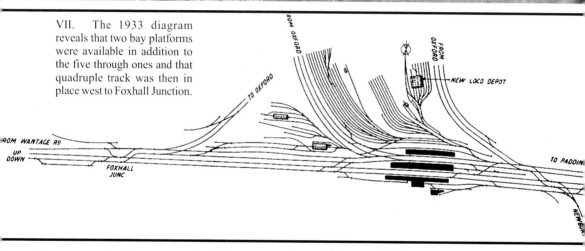

VII. The 1933 diagram reveals that two bay platforms were available in addition to the five through ones and that quadruple track was then in place west to Foxhall Junction.

4.   No. 7001 *Sir James Milne* was recorded with a Paddington to Cheltenham service in the mid-1950s. Also evident is the down bay and West End box, which was in use until 17th May 1965 and had 88 levers. (Rev. A.W.V.Mace/Milepost 92½ Picture Library)

5.   No. 6027 *King Richard I* stands with eleven coaches bound for Paddington in misty weather on 8th January 1962. On the left is the bay used by trains bound for Newbury and Winchester until that service was withdrawn in 1964. (M.A.N.Johnston)

6.   An up ballast train runs onto Chester Line Junction on 14th September 1974, hauled by no. 25152. Obscured partially by the rear wagons is the former Tranship Shed, once used for the transfer of goods between wagons of different gauges. (T.Heavyside)

7.   Standing on the sidings north of the platforms on 30th March 1975 was a class 08 diesel shunter, two class 47s and a "Brush Type 2" diesel of class 31. The coal is destined for the power station, the cooling towers of which appear in the background. The fence marks the boundary of the Didcot Railway Centre which made plans to acquire these sidings 25 years later. (R.Ruffell/M.J.Stretton)

8.   The station was given the suffix "Parkway" when the new building on the right was opened on 29th July 1985. The 16.45 Paddington to Bristol is seen on 22nd June 1990 at platform 1. This had been numbered 3 until 1965, when the bays were closed. Visitors to the Didcot Railway Centre enter on the right, pass through the subway and use the foot crossing on the left. (M.J.Stretton)

9.   Approaching the station on 25th September 1996 and passing under the footbridge to the massive car park is a train loaded with coal imported via Avonmouth and destined for the power station in the background. The line for trains to Oxford is to the right of no. 60073. (M.J.Stretton)

10.   A new diesel depot opened at the west end of the triangle in April 1994. It undertook refuelling, inspection and minor repairs to freight locomotives. Outside on 26th September 1996 is no. 37413 *Loch Eil Outward Bound*. (M.J.Stretton)

Other Middleton Press albums to feature this station include *Didcot to Winchester* and *Reading to Didcot*.

WEST OF DIDCOT

11.   A "Castle" 4-6-0 speeds east with an express from Cardiff in the mid-1950s, having just passed Foxhall Junction box. This was open from 13th October 1931 until 17th May 1965 and it had 76 levers. Its predecessor had been in the vee of the junction with West Curve.
(Rev. A.W.V.Mace/Milepost 92½ Picture Library)

12.   Class 4700 2-8-0 no. 4703 passes the six-ton crane and the mighty provender store on 22nd September 1961. It is running on the "Up Main", the "Down Main" being on the right. These had been "Down Main" and "Down Goods" respectively from 1899 to 1931. (M.Mensing/M.J.Stretton)

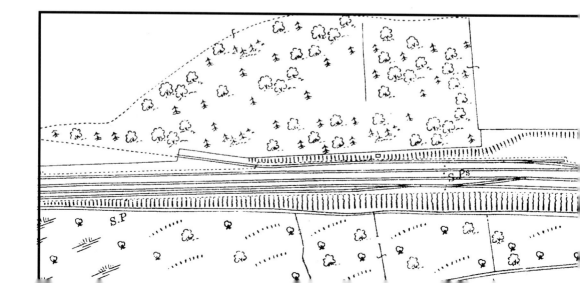

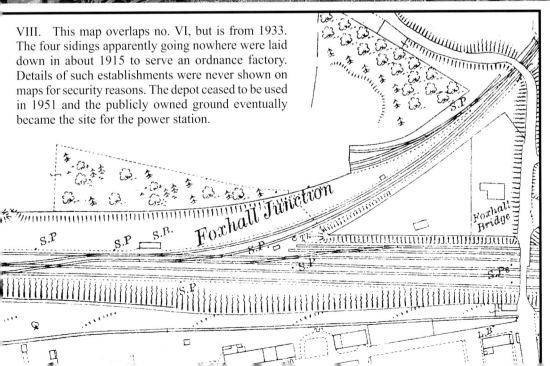

VIII. This map overlaps no. VI, but is from 1933. The four sidings apparently going nowhere were laid down in about 1915 to serve an ordnance factory. Details of such establishments were never shown on maps for security reasons. The depot ceased to be used in 1951 and the publicly owned ground eventually became the site for the power station.

Foxhall Junction

Foxhall Bridge

S.P
S.P
S.B.
S.P
S.P
S.P
S.P
S.P

13.   Didcot station is in the distance as no. 47232 runs on the "Down Relief" with coal for the power station on 3rd October 1975. The Tranship Shed in the background was transferred in sections to the Didcot Railway Centre in 1977 and one side of it now has broad gauge track again. (T.Heavyside)

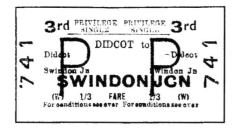

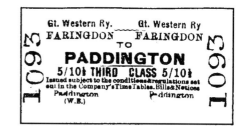

14.   Coal supply to the power station began in September 1969, it coming from pits in the Midlands for many years. Two loops were provided to the coal discharge point and another for ash loading, allowing merry-go-round continuous operation. No. 56049 is leaving with empties on 19th June 1982. (M.Turvey)

15.   The previous photograph was taken from the far side of the bridge, under which the arrival lines are on the left. *King Edward I* is seen on 2nd October 1996 hauling the "25th Anniversary Limited", which commemorated the "Return to Steam" tour of 1971. The bright rails to the right of the locomotive are those of the "Up Relief", the dull ones having earlier served the Milton Freight Terminal. (S.P.Derek)

16.   Moving to the other side of the bridge, we see the same train crossing to take the "Down West Curve", on its way to Birmingham Snow Hill. As it had done 25 years earlier, the train had started at Hereford and ran via the Severn Tunnel. (S.P.Derek)

17.   An up HST passes the site of the goods yard and provender mill in June 1990, having just passed under Foxhall Bridge. Its steel span dates from the widening of 1931. The reason for the suffix "Parkway" is now evident. (M.J.Stretton)

18.   No. 66235 is hauling a train of the new HTA wagons on the "Down Relief" on 1st November 2001. They are being returned from the power station in the background to Avonmouth. Milton signal box, which had 35 levers, had been on the left from 12th April 1942 to 1st December 1963. Its predecessor was ¾ mile further west. Obscured by the trees are the five sidings that were opened on the Milton Trading Estate on 16th May 1974. (S.P.McMullin)

←——

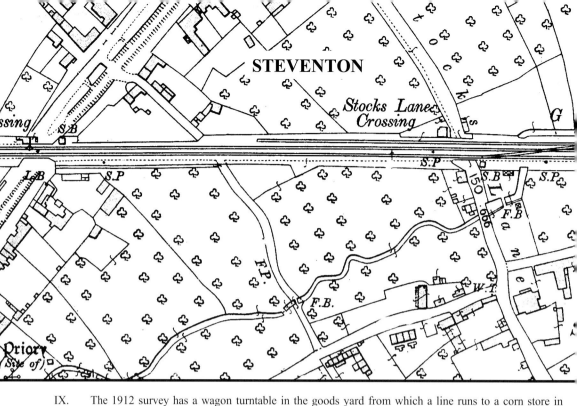

IX.   The 1912 survey has a wagon turntable in the goods yard from which a line runs to a corn store in Booker's orchard. The top line on the right is the 1907 up goods line to Foxhall Junction. The down goods line was completed in 1916.

19.   An early 20th century postcard includes the signal and points for the up goods loop. The station served as a terminus for seven weeks, but more importantly it was the station for Oxford for four years, until it had its own station. There was usually a staff here of 14 between the wars. (Lens of Sutton)

20.   A 1919 westward view includes the weighbridge office, right. The goods shed had a one-ton crane and the yard was in use until 29th March 1965. The signal box seen here closed on 1st April 1928 and was replaced by one to the left of the level crossing in the distance. That one had 36 levers and lasted until 12th May 1965. Thereafter, it simply controlled crossing gates until full lifting barriers arrived in 1972. Causeway Crossing (left on the map) was staffed from then on to work both sets of barriers. (LGRP/NRM)

F.B.

Br o o k

B
ge

Goods Shed   Cattle Pen   W.M   Station   S.P.

Vulcan Iron Wor

GRE.

S.B   S.P

ine Farm

Spring

Steventon	1903	1913	1923	1933
Passenger tickets issued	10747	12512	12060	4357
Season tickets issued	*	*	17	4
Parcels forwarded	6804	9652	6358	4991
General goods forwarded (tons)	4913	4124	4599	899
Coal and coke received (tons)	-	277	315	420
Other minerals received (tons)	2262	9806	6344	2322
General goods received (tons)	2389	6395	1544	1461
Trucks of livestock handled	34	43	46	25

(* not available.)

21.   Beyond the bridge are the two goods lines, the down one being a little over one mile long, whereas the up is 2½ miles in length and, like the main lines, reversible nowadays. The bridge then carried the Oxford-Southampton road, numbered A34 since 1919. The station closed to passengers on 7th December 1964, when the local population was slightly over 1000. (Lens of Sutton)

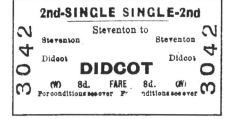

22.   The station was almost half way between Paddington and Bristol. Thus, the house on the right of picture 20 was used for GWR board meetings in the early years. Later, the local inn took up the claim and a genuine GWR signal was erected. It is seen in 1994. There had been four loop lines on the north of the main lines, west of the station from 1940 to 1950 for War Department traffic. (M.J.Stretton)

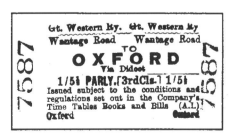

WANTAGE ROAD

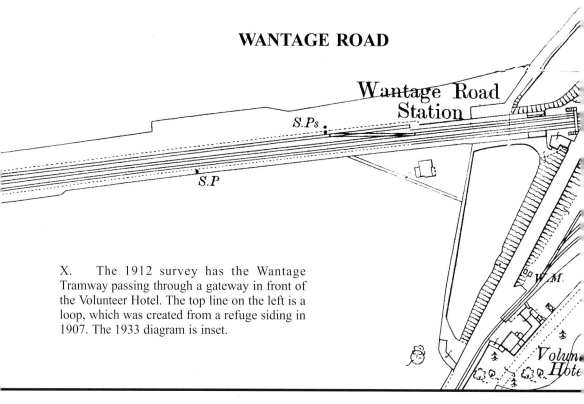

Wantage Road
Station

S.Ps

S.P

X.   The 1912 survey has the Wantage
Tramway passing through a gateway in front of
the Volunteer Hotel. The top line on the left is a
loop, which was created from a refuge siding in
1907. The 1933 diagram is inset.

W.M.

*Volun.
Hote*

23.   Features of note in this postcard view are the three storeys of the main building and the
longitudinal timbers of the loop, a design employed almost universally on broad gauge track. The
brick arch of the road bridge is partially obscured by the footbridge seen in picture 27.
(Lens of Sutton)

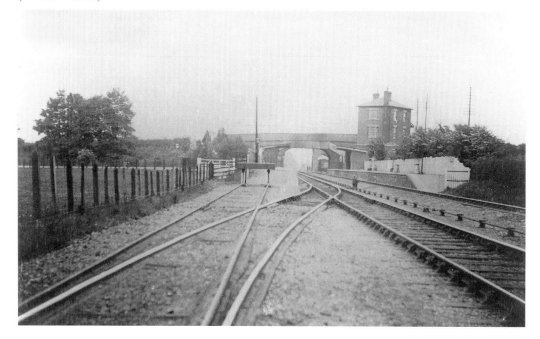

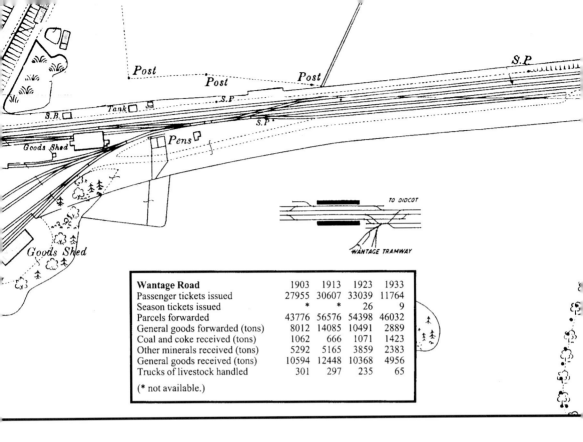

Wantage Road	1903	1913	1923	1933
Passenger tickets issued	27955	30607	33039	11764
Season tickets issued	*	*	26	9
Parcels forwarded	43776	56576	54398	46032
General goods forwarded (tons)	8012	14085	10491	2889
Coal and coke received (tons)	1062	666	1071	1423
Other minerals received (tons)	5292	5165	3859	2383
General goods received (tons)	10594	12448	10368	4956
Trucks of livestock handled	301	297	235	65

(* not available.)

24.   Another indifferent postcard is included as it shows the platform shelters more clearly and also some of the staff. There were 17 men employed here in 1903. (Lens of Sutton)

25.   Quadruple track came into use from here for 3½ miles westward late in 1932, the signal box opening on 7th October. Its predecessor (built in 1915) had stood on the site of the new up lines. The down line in the distance had been slewed to connect with the old up line, which became the through track for down trains. The photograph is from 1933. (Brunel University/Mowat coll.)

26.   An eastbound goods was recorded behind 2-8-0T no. 4288 on 17th June 1939. The brake van of this typical slow freight is near Circourt signal box which was in use from 1915 to 1954 and had 24 levers. It was about half way along the quadruple section to Challow. (H.C.Casserley)

27.   The chalked word NOT had inevitably been erased by observers of railway practice. The edict was particularly inept as exhibited on this platform was the Wantage Tramway's 0-4-0 WT no. 5 *Shannon*. The station closed to passengers on 7th December 1964. (Lens of Sutton)

28.   The goods yard and its 12-ton crane were photographed in March 1957, twelve years after the last freight had trundled through the foreground on the tramway to Wantage. The yard closed on 29th March 1965 and the 61-lever signal box in the background followed two months later. (R.M.Casserley)

29.   This bridge replaced the one seen in picture 23 and carries the A338. Both of the long loops to Challow were taken out of use on 5th April 1965 and subsequently lifted. This May 1992 view from the old down platform shows reinstatement in progress. (M.J.Stretton)

30.   No. 37342 takes the down relief line on 5th February 1997, with engineers empties from Didcot to Swindon. A new crossover is being assembled in the former goods yard. (S.P.McMullin)

31.   An HST speeds towards London on 17th June 2000. No. 4936 *Kinlet Hall* waits at the end of the up relief line with a train on a circular tour from Birmingham via Worcester and Didcot. Both the main lines were signalled for reversible running. (M.Turvey)

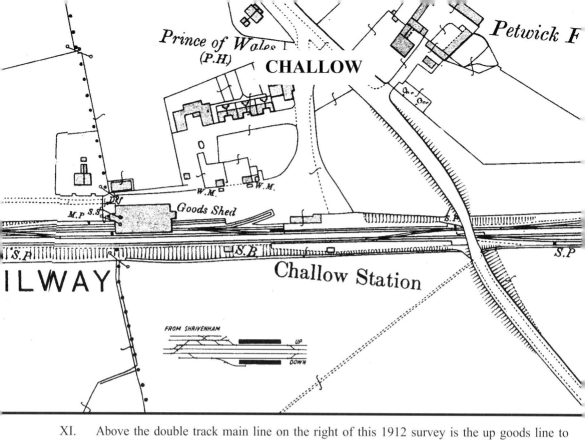

Prince of Wales (P.H.)

CHALLOW

Petwick F

W.M.   W.M.

Goods Shed

M.P. S.S.

S.B.

S.P.

S.P.

ILWAY

Challow Station

FROM SHRIVENHAM

UP

DOWN

XI.   Above the double track main line on the right of this 1912 survey is the up goods line to Wantage Road, completed in 1907. The lower track was a refuge siding from 1898 to 1932, when it became part of the down relief line. Inset is the 1933 track diagram.

32.   A 1919 westward view features the massive goods shed, the doorways of which unusually accommodated two tracks. There was a staff of 10 to 12 men from then until 1938. The station had been "Faringdon Road" until 1st June 1864. (LGRP/NRM)

33.   The quadrupling from Wantage Road was completed on 22nd January 1933 and the new platforms are seen shortly afterwards. A new building of brick instead of timber was provided nearer to the main road. (LGRP/NRM)

34.   No. 6961 *Stedham Hall* is seen with a westbound express on 26th April 1959. The circular objects on the posts were winches for hoisting pressurised oil lights, known by their trade name of "Tilley". They were first tried by the GWR at this station in about 1925 and were thus often described by railwaymen as "Challows". (H.C.Casserley)

Challow	1903	1913	1923	1933
Passenger tickets issued	10034	11691	11259	6801
Season tickets issued	*	*	39	5
Parcels forwarded	54856	64423	59408	41367
General goods forwarded (tons)	3858	3781	2879	813
Coal and coke received (tons)	319	373	270	128
Other minerals received (tons)	4248	5594	5013	4652
General goods received (tons)	3630	3777	3027	2186
Trucks of livestock handled	133	370	245	49
(* not available.)				

35. Ex-GWR 0-6-0ST no. 1365 was an unusual visitor and is seen on the same day, returning with a special train from Faringdon. The 63-lever signal box was in use from 4th December 1932 until 30th June 1965. Passenger services were withdrawn on 7th December 1964 and goods traffic ceased on 29th March 1965. (D.Lawrence)

36. A fragment of up platform is evident as nos. 37371 and 37350 roar west with empty tankers from Theale to Robeston (Milford Haven) on 9th February 1989. The loop lines from Wantage Road had gone soon after being taken out of use in April 1965. (M.J.Stretton)

37. Running east on 12th December 1992 were nos. 47673 *Galloway Princess*, 47675 *Confederation of British Industry* and 47626, then un-named. Work in the foreground is in connection with provision of points for the down relief line. The platform on the right would soon go, to make way for the up points. (S.P.McMullin)

UFFINGTON

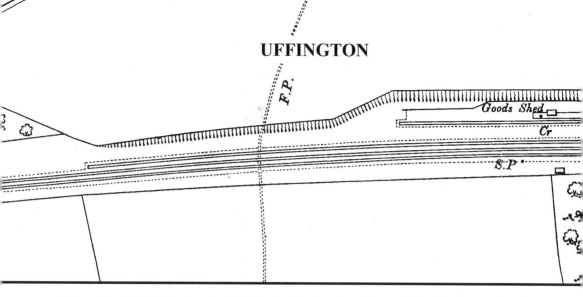

XII.   The 1912 edition has the 1864 Faringdon branch at the top. There had been a level crossing to the left of the footbridge until 1897.

38.   An 1897 postcard includes many of the staff, usually numbering eight in the early years of the next century. The Faringdon branch is on the left and the milk churns stand on the site of an earlier goods shed. Oil lamps are evident; pressurised ones came in 1926 and electricity arrived in 1962. (M.J.Stretton coll.)

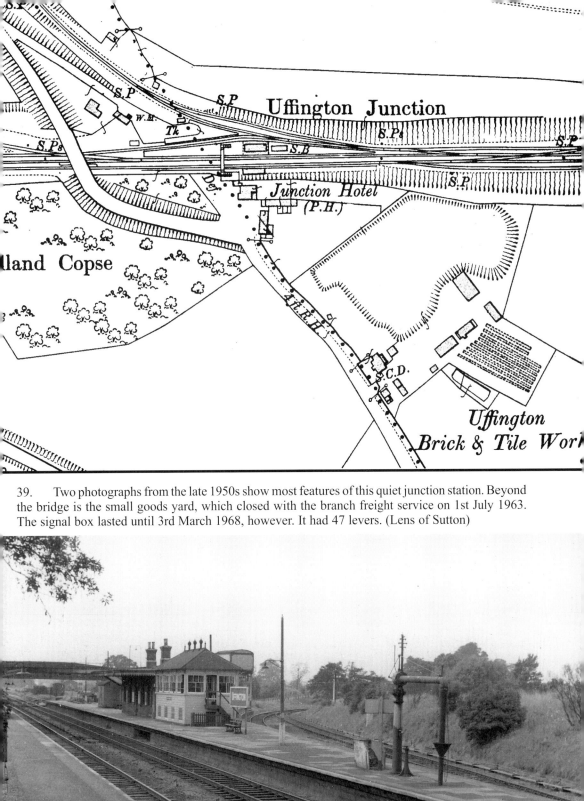

39.   Two photographs from the late 1950s show most features of this quiet junction station. Beyond the bridge is the small goods yard, which closed with the branch freight service on 1st July 1963. The signal box lasted until 3rd March 1968, however. It had 47 levers. (Lens of Sutton)

40.　The loop on the left was not signalled for passenger trains, but was convenient for shunting the two goods sidings. There was a goods platform which had a small shed and a 30cwt crane. The population of Uffington was under 600 during the life of the station. (Lens of Sutton)

→

41.　The Railway Enthusiasts Club's special from Faringdon on 26th April 1959 was recorded while no. 1365 took water. The locomotive was later scrapped, but sister 1363 can be seen at the Didcot Railway Centre. The station closed to passengers on 7th December 1964. (R.M.Casserley)

Uffington	1903	1913	1923	1933
Passenger tickets issued	12162	10996	9489	6260
Season tickets issued	*	*	6	5
Parcels forwarded	30834	35142	31829	9007
General goods forwarded (tons)	498	639	789	138
Coal and coke received (tons)	32	75	46	92
Other minerals received (tons)	1064	1557	1753	380
General goods received (tons)	937	863	1124	449
Trucks of livestock handled	-	-	1	5

(* not available.)

→

42.　Two photographs from 8th August 1993 show the site of the station. Points are being assembled on the land once occupied by the goods yard. These up and down loops had been brought into use on 7th March 1962. (M.J.Stretton)

43.　　The roof on the right has been seen earlier in picture 38, when it was part of the Junction Hotel. The new crossovers were of larger radius to allow running at higher speeds. The loops were subsequently taken out of use. (M.J.Stretton)

44.　　The bridge shown in pictures 39 and 41 is seen being dismantled on 25th January 1997, its centenary year. It carried a minor road - see next map. Fullers Earth is dug in this area, but none is conveyed by rail. It is used in the chemical industry and for cat litter. (M.J.Stretton)

45.　　The replacement structure was recorded on 21st April 1997, as no. 37505 was hauling a down freight service under it. The length was the same, although there were then only two lines in use, both bidirectional. (M.J.Stretton)

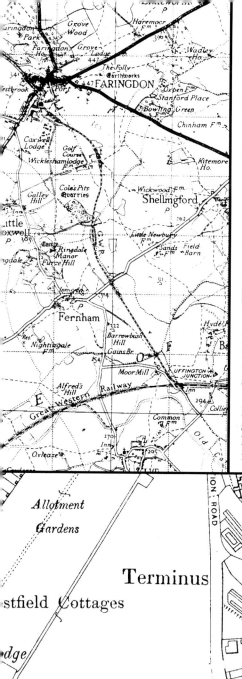

Faringdon Branch

FARINGDON

Faringdon	1903	1913	1923	1933
Passenger tickets issued	18052	19023	14051	4569
Season tickets issued	*	*	5	6
Parcels forwarded	62585	65166	78157	24154
General goods forwarded (tons)	3249	3594	3371	993
Coal and coke received (tons)	752	1140	1454	553
Other minerals received (tons)	3729	3735	11023	5227
General goods received (tons)	7573	8136	5987	5321
Trucks of livestock handled	259	491	343	55

(* not available.)

XIII. The 1947 map at 1ins to 1 mile includes the entire 3½ mile long branch and also Uffington village. Its population fell from about 3700 when the line opened to 2900 at the turn of the century, rising to 3389 in 1961.

XIV. The terminus is shown on the 1912 survey as modified after the GWR took over the local company in 1886. The former had undertaken the conversion of the branch to standard gauge in July 1878.

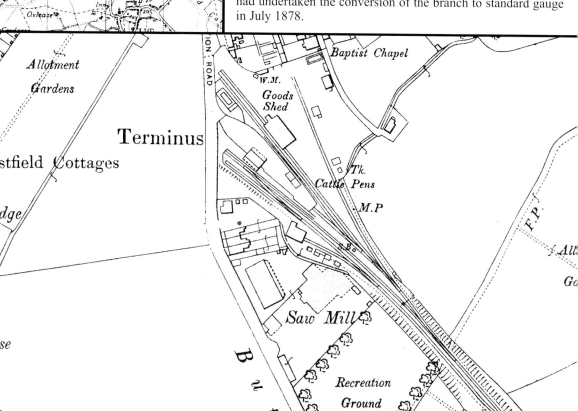

46.   A faded postcard is the earliest view we can offer. It has the engine shed and water tank on the left and the signal box in the centre. It had six levers and had initially been to the left of the tracks. Many passengers were lost when bus competition arrived in 1923. (Lens of Sutton)

47.   This poor picture is included to illustrate one of the important commodities loaded here. There was a through milk van to Paddington at 6.15pm for many years. Note the modern low floor cart for this traffic. (Lens of Sutton)

48. A 1919 panorama not only includes contemporary travel apparel, but shows two female labourers. These would soon be dismissed, as they were required only during wartime. The locomotive is running round and has just passed a GE wagon. There were eight men engaged here in the mid-1930s. (LGRP/NRM)

49. No. 4697 has just arrived with brake/composite no. W7693 on 24th December 1951, six days before withdrawal of passenger service. The signal box in the background had served only as a ground frame since 1934. (J.H.Meredith)

50. A few minutes later, the same train was photographed, despite the weather. The carriage appears to be a former slip coach. Note that the lighting had been modernised when compared with picture 48. (J.H.Meredith)

51. The Southall Railway Club hired railcar no. W16 for a visit to the branch in April 1955. This gives us a close view of one of the quaint ornamental buttresses that adorned the four corners of the building. (RAS Marketing)

52. Four photographs from the late 1950s follow. This features the crane which was rated at six tons capacity, higher than all but one on the main line. The siding on the right was a GWR addition. (J.H.Moss/R.S.Carpenter)

53. The engine shed was closed in 1933 and subsequently the branch engine came from Swindon each day. The building was used as a dairy for some years. (J.H.Moss/R.S.Carpenter)

54.   The charming building with gullied roof seems to have lost its symmetry with the insertion of an oversize sash window. Not only were all the buildings constructed of stone (600 tons were used), but so were the cattle pens, left. (J.H.Moss/R.S.Carpenter)

55.   There was also symmetry on the south elevation with two Gothic arched doorways, one for the pleasure of gentlemen and the other for the lamp man. The GWR usually had a lamp hut remote from other buildings for fire risk reasons. (R.M.Casserley)

56.   The REC special shown in pictures 35 and 41 is seen after running round at its destination on 6th April 1959. The building was in use as a SCATS shop in 2002. (D.Lawrence)

57.   The final special train was operated on 9th April 1961 by the RCTS using a class 120 DMU. Freight traffic continued until 1st July 1963 and the site is now occupied by various commercial premises. (F.Hornby)

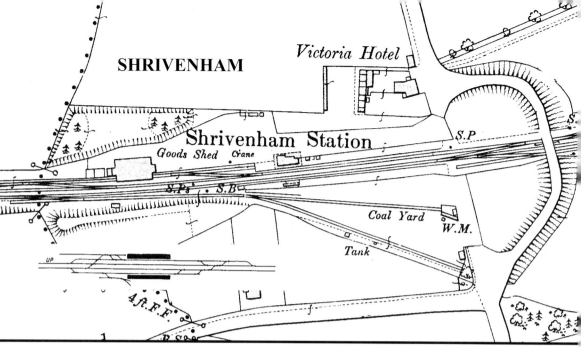

SHRIVENHAM

Victoria Hotel

Shrivenham Station

Goods Shed Crane

S.P.

S.Ps. • *S.B.*

Coal Yard

W.M.

Tank

UP

4 *R. F. F.*

XV.   On the right of this 1912 edition is the 1904 up loop and the 1903 down one. The former extended to Knighton Crossing (1½ miles) and the latter to Ashbury Crossing (½ mile). They were taken out of use in 1966-67 and 1962 respectively, their boxes having 10 and 31 levers, respectively. Two ambulance train sidings branched from the up loop between 1944 and 1949. The inset 1933 diagram has the loops on the right; they were connected to quadruple track through the station in May of that year. The new signal box had 50 levers and lasted until 5th June 1966.

58.   This eastward view from soon after the 1933 alterations reveals that the old up platform was retained and lengthened. The down platform was new, although the Pagoda shelter seems to be of some age. The signal box was behind the camera. The bridge carried the B4000. Two lives were lost on 15th January 1936 when *King William III,* working the overnight train from Penzance, collided with some detached wagons near Ashbury Crossing. (LGRP/NRM)

59.	The up platform retained its brick building with stone quoins. The local population rose from 633 in 1901 to 2016 in 1961, but passenger services ceased on 7th December 1964. Up to 20 men were employed here in the 1930s. (Lens of Sutton)

60.	The up platform is evident as Sprinter no. 150278 works the once-a-day service from Swindon to Oxford on 18th April 1990. The land in the background had accommodated the goods yard until its closure on 4th October 1965. Nearby is the Royal Military College of Science. Three loop lines with four parallel sidings were laid down two miles west of the station in 1942. Named Marston, they lasted until 1962-66 and had signal boxes with 30 and 37 levers. (M.J.Stretton)

WEST OF SHRIVENHAM

61.   The South Marston Euroterminal Keypoint was under construction when the 09.30 from Swansea was recorded on 2nd February 2000, with no. 43033 leading. The points were connected (but not used) in April 2002. Traffic from Europe was disrupted owing to the Government's failure to exercise its right to employ the Army to prevent the invasion of the UK by aliens, or even threaten to use it. (S.P.McMullin)

TO DIDCOT

Shrivenham	1903	1913	1923	1933
Passenger tickets issued	16303	17245	14547	7287
Season tickets issued	*	*	43	52
Parcels forwarded	61440	67148	56414	19051
General goods forwarded (tons)	2016	1670	1586	337
Coal and coke received (tons)	293	306	228	413
Other minerals received (tons)	2767	2508	7834	2391
General goods received (tons)	2814	3112	2022	1632
Trucks of livestock handled	292	442	277	57
(* not available.)				

Keypoint track diagram as announced by the developer.

TO SWINDON

STRATTON PARK HALT

62.   As the residential area of Swindon had spread eastwards, a halt was opened here on 20th November 1933. It was on the east of the B4021 (later A419), at the south end of Stratton St. Margaret. Initially there was only one train calling; this was at 5.49pm, weekdays only, starting from Swindon. The halt closed on 7th December 1964, by which time there were three down trains and two up, weekdays only. (Lens of Sutton)

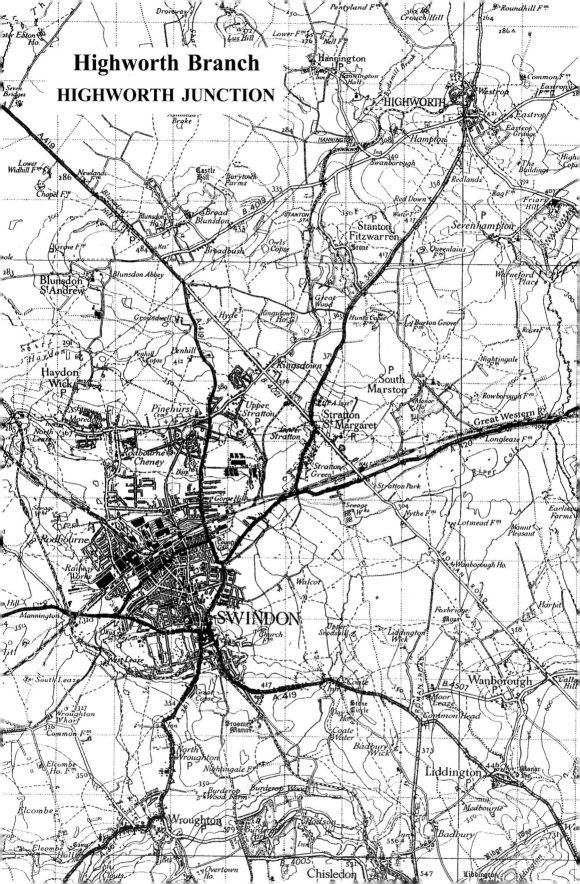

Highworth Branch

HIGHWORTH JUNCTION

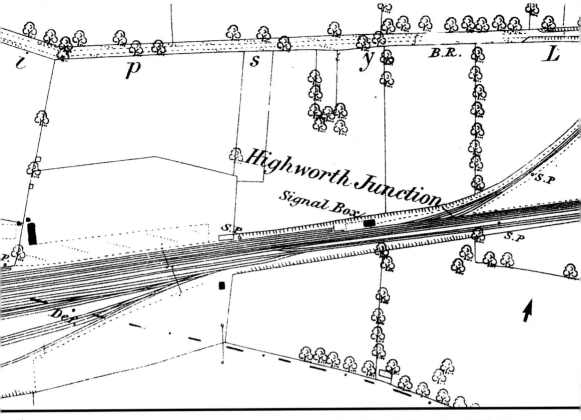

XVI. The 1947 revision of the 1ins to 1 mile survey has the branch terminus top right. The main line runs across the page and the location of Stratton Park Halt is shown. The line meandering diagonally down the left side of the page for Chisledon is featured in our *Cheltenham to Andover* album and was part of the Midland & South Western Junction Railway until 1923. It crosses the Gloucester branch, north of the Bristol line.

XVII. The first edition is from about 1886 when the cartographer had the problem of showing three rails on the dual gauge tracks. The Highworth branch single line curves on the right, while the Swindon goods yard spreads out lower left. It is still known as "Swindon Transfer", as there was once a transhipment shed of the type seen at Didcot.

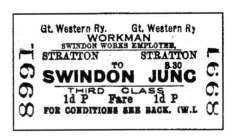

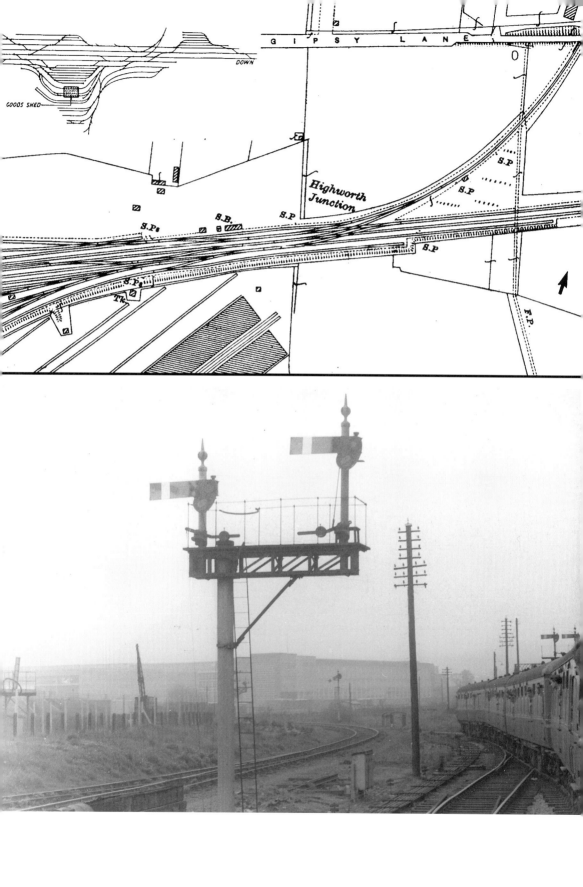

XVIII. The 1923 survey includes a siding (left upper) to the gasworks, added in 1913. Radstock coal was used for many years; the works closed in 1968. The sidings near the lower border were provided for a munitions works in World War I and were used afterwards by the Imperial Tobacco Company to produce an alternative method of dying. Their sidings were in use until 29th October 1980. The inset diagram is from 1933.

63.   The junction was recorded on 9th April 1961 from a DMU running onto the branch while carrying an RCTS party. Only the track on the left remained as a connection to the branch on 31st May 1964. The 80-lever signal box is to the left of the camera and it closed on 3rd March 1968. (A.E.Bennett)

64.   The branch is on the right as 47375 *Tinsley Traction Depot* and 47280 *Pedigree* run on the "Up Reception" on 5th February 1997, having just run round their train of car panels prior to departure for Longbridge. RFD class 66 locomotives took over this work early in 1999. (S.P.McMullin)

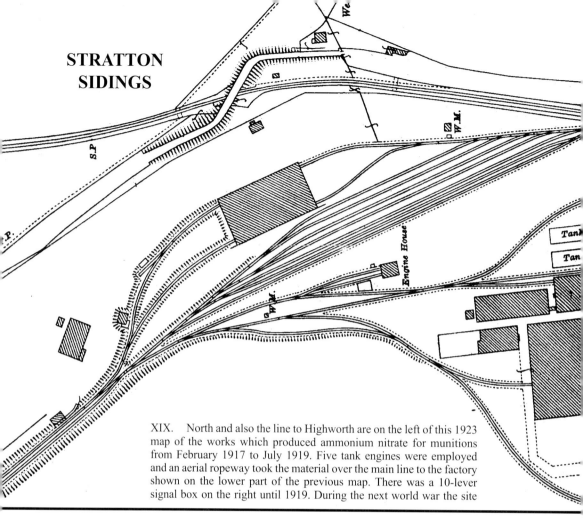

STRATTON SIDINGS

XIX.   North and also the line to Highworth are on the left of this 1923 map of the works which produced ammonium nitrate for munitions from February 1917 to July 1919. Five tank engines were employed and an aerial ropeway took the material over the main line to the factory shown on the lower part of the previous map. There was a 10-lever signal box on the right until 1919. During the next world war the site

65.   A northward view in March 1993 features the body panel plant and some of the sidings thereto. The two being removed had been laid in about 1960, as had the six in the distance. The turnout on the left is on the site of the one shown on the right of the map and served Coopers, scrap metal processors. It was still in use in 2002. (M.J.Stretton)

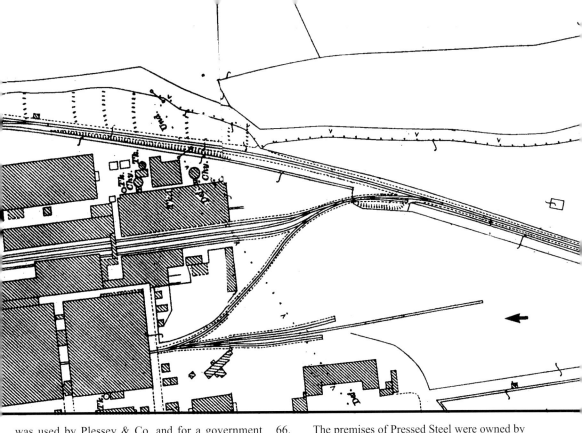

was used by Plessey & Co. and for a government Reserve Supply Depot. A siding came into use on the east side of the branch in 1958 for The Pressed Steel Company, which had produced bodies for motor cars here since 1955. The first were for Daimlers, Hillmans and Sprites.

66.   The premises of Pressed Steel were owned by Rover when no. 47323 *Rover Group, Quality Assured* crept round one of the sharp curves of the internal system on 23rd February 1994, the day that it was so named. No bodies were produced after 1980, all the consignments being panels stacked in racks.
(M.J.Stretton)

67.   The end of the branch since 1965 is in the left distance in this photograph from May 1994. The remains of the four north sidings are left of centre and no. 396 *Le Manis* is beyond the level crossing, on one of the three lines leading to the northern group of tracks of the Rover complex. (M.J.Stretton)

68.   The first siding for scrap metal was put in here in about 1956 and by 2000 it was operated by European Metal Recycling. No doubt many panels were produced on the left of the track to eventually end up on the right. No. 08644 is shunting PXAs on 13th September 1995. Much of the scrap travelled to Hamworthy for export, via Cardiff. (S.P.McMullin)

69.   Having passed under Gypsy Lane, no. 47316 arrives with empty Cargowaggons from Longbridge on 9th May 1994. The scrap metal sidings are on the right. The press tools from the massive body shop at Cowley were moved here in 1993, greatly increasing output. (M.J.Stretton)

70.   Fowler diesels no. 4220017 and 4220032 wait inside the Rover complex for their next duties on the same day. Back in 1982 a fleet of six Fowlers was kept here. (M.J.Stretton)

71.   There were eight loading lines at the plant in the 1960s. This one is near the centre of the site in 1994. Other cars to have been conceived here are Triumphs, MGs, Allegros, Metros and so on. (M.J.Stretton)

72.   Designated KSAA, this wagon was new when photographed on 2nd April 1996. Note the mid-way well and stacking frames. The nearby Honda factory has been supplied from this plant since 1992, but it does not involve rail transport. (M.J.Stretton)

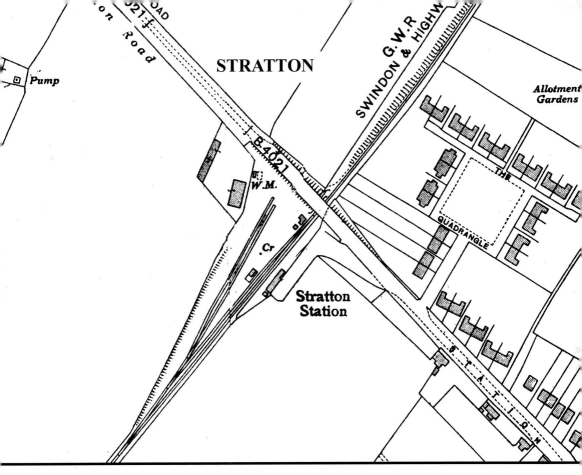

STRATTON

Pump

Allotment Gardens

B4021

W.M.

Cr

Stratton Station

QUADRANGLE

THE

G.W.R SWINDON & HIGHW

STATION

XX.   The station was 1¼ miles from the junction and is seen on the 1941 map. The site is now occupied by factories and the bridge was removed in the 1970s. Station Road is on the alignment of the Roman Ermine Street.

73.   Swindon is in the left background as we look down from the road bridge in around 1920 at the extensive collection of barrows. There were four men here for most of the 1920s and three in the 1930s. The profusion of trolleys reflects the significance of milk traffic here. (LGRP/NRM)

74.   Behind the 3-ton crane in this later view in indifferent weather is the Trinidad Asphalt plant. There had been a signal box on the site of the platform extension until 1909. Arkell's brewery generated traffic inwards in the form of hops, malt, sugar and coal. (Lens of Sutton)

75.   This 1952 panorama includes evidence of track lifting. The second siding, on which the wagon is standing, was added in about 1909. Goods traffic ceased on 4th October 1965, most of the line northwards having closed three years earlier. The rodding tunnel had once served a ground frame. (H.C.Casserley)

76.   The parcels shed was showing signs of decay towards the end of its life and only one of the two Rochester style gas lamps remained. The Windsor model, seen in the previous picture, had also vanished. Arkell's beer had once been despatched from here. (Lens of Sutton)

Stratton	1903	1913	1923	1933
Passenger tickets issued	28042	21521	20114	2521
Season tickets issued	*	*	475	313
Parcels forwarded	21772	31830	41845	14015
General goods forwarded (tons)	326	623	661	381
Coal and coke received (tons)	463	348	197	527
Other minerals received (tons)	2249	3140	2333	10789
General goods received (tons)	2730	1820	2303	906
Trucks of livestock handled	-	-	-	-

(* not available.)

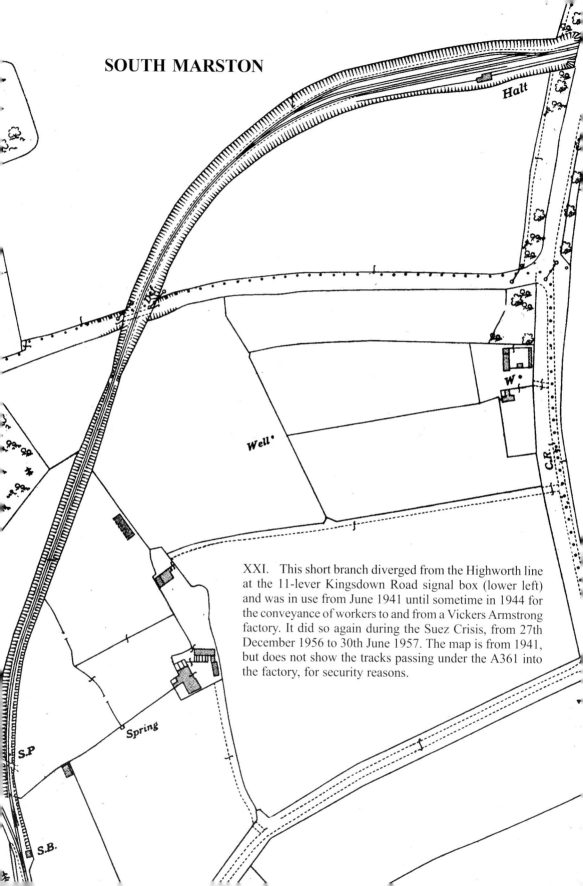

SOUTH MARSTON

Halt

Well

W

C.P.

Well

Spring

S.P.

S.B.

XXI.   This short branch diverged from the Highworth line at the 11-lever Kingsdown Road signal box (lower left) and was in use from June 1941 until sometime in 1944 for the conveyance of workers to and from a Vickers Armstrong factory. It did so again during the Suez Crisis, from 27th December 1956 to 30th June 1957. The map is from 1941, but does not show the tracks passing under the A361 into the factory, for security reasons.

77. Two photographs from 27th April 1961 show the track still in use, as it served the factory until line closure on 24th June 1965. Kingsdown Road box opened on 17th February 1942 and a ground frame was provided outside it on 19th June 1958. (M.A.N.Johnston)

78. Bright rails were to be seen from the Highworth Road. Two loops, three docks and an engine shed were provided in the works. No public service was offered. The factory produced aircraft, notably Spitfires. The cutting was later infilled, burying the platform for future archaeologists. (M.A.N.Johnston)

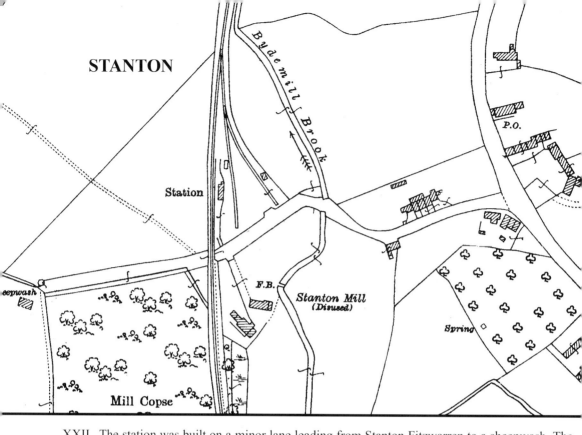

STANTON

Station

Stanton Mill
(Disused)

Mill Copse

XXII. The station was built on a minor lane leading from Stanton Fitzwarren to a sheepwash. The brook runs north to flow into the River Thames near Lechlade.

79.   This peaceful rural location was recorded on 6th September 1952, six months before public passenger services ceased. There were three people on the payroll here in 1923, but from 1929 to 1949, when staffing ceased, there was only one. The points to the yard are in the distance; one of the two sidings had been removed in 1925. (H.C.Casserley)

80.   The goods yard closed on 1st March 1953 and the remaining siding was lifted in 1958. In its final years, one goods and two workmens trains passed each way every weekday. (Lens of Sutton)

Stanton	1903	1913	1923	1933
Passenger tickets issued	2968	2384	3666	533
Season tickets issued	*	*	22	14
Parcels forwarded	7798	11655	7785	1767
General goods forwarded (tons)	82	66	46	6
Coal and coke received (tons)	-	-	9	-
Other minerals received (tons)	308	315	137	246
General goods received (tons)	189	295	223	52
Trucks of livestock handled	-	-	-	3
(* not available.)				

NORTH OF STANTON

81.   The 1.20pm from Highworth stops for the gates on the Cricklade road to be opened on 6th September 1952. The 0-4-2T is no. 5804. (H.C.Casserley)

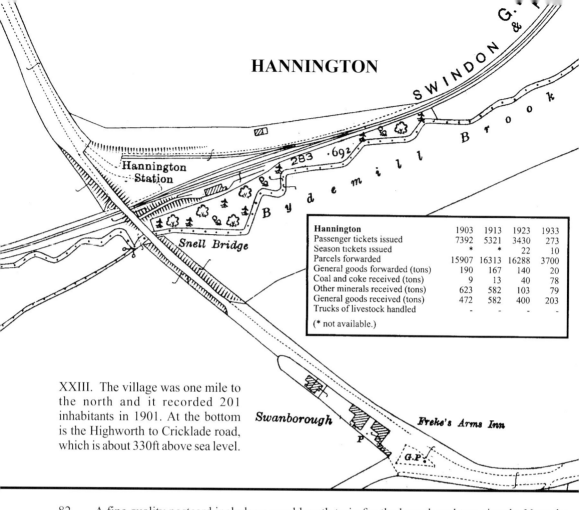

HANNINGTON

Hannington Station

Snell Bridge

283 .692

SWINDON G&

Bydemill Brook

Hannington	1903	1913	1923	1933
Passenger tickets issued	7392	5321	3430	273
Season tickets issued	*	*	22	10
Parcels forwarded	15907	16313	16288	3700
General goods forwarded (tons)	190	167	140	20
Coal and coke received (tons)	9	13	40	78
Other minerals received (tons)	623	582	103	79
General goods received (tons)	472	582	400	203
Trucks of livestock handled	-	-	-	-
(* not available.)				

XXIII. The village was one mile to the north and it recorded 201 inhabitants in 1901. At the bottom is the Highworth to Cricklade road, which is about 330ft above sea level.

Swanborough

Freke's Arms Inn

G.P.

82. A fine quality postcard includes a good length train for the branch and two signals. Note the splendid gardens near the open door. (Lens of Sutton)

83.   A rodding tunnel under the platform indicates the location of the signal box. It stood on the right until 1910. There was only one man here after 1923. The photograph is from 1952. (H.C.Casserley)

84.   An April 1961 record shows that one lamp was retained for the benefit of returning workmen. The sidings were not used after 1959. (M.A.N.Johnston)

HIGHWORTH

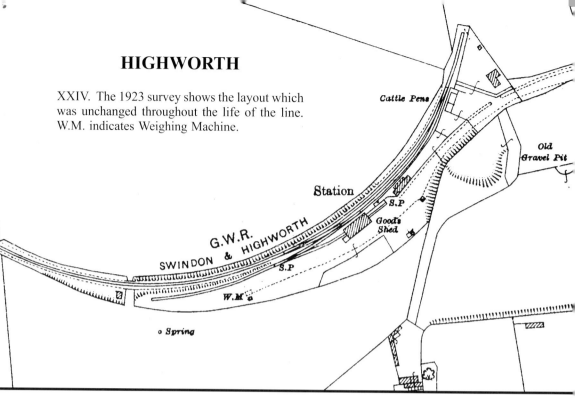

XXIV. The 1923 survey shows the layout which was unchanged throughout the life of the line. W.M. indicates Weighing Machine.

Highworth	1903	1913	1923	1933
Passenger tickets issued	32390	24388	13314	4402
Season tickets issued	*	*	282	187
Parcels forwarded	34449	40692	40832	22187
General goods forwarded (tons)	643	984	1081	988
Coal and coke received (tons)	361	628	774	456
Other minerals received (tons)	1624	2014	236	1749
General goods received (tons)	3772	3001	3132	1454
Trucks of livestock handled	86	81	145	16

(* not available.)

85.   This once splendid photograph has been spoilt in the copying. Its composition involved moving the train back towards the buffers. The sign on the signal box reads "Highworth Ground Frame", which dates the view as after 1910. (Lens of Sutton)

86.　Three photographs from 1951 reveal the topography. This shows the cattle dock, which could only be used between trains. On the left is the lamp hut. There was an average of five men here in the 1930s. (J.H.Moss/R.S.Carpenter)

87.　The climb into the station is evident, as the goods yard is level. Notable amongst goods outward were mats and carpets from the Vorda Works and agricultural equipment from Bartrops. The latter sent 36 tons of horseshoes in one week during World War I. Goods inward thus included coconut fibre and steel, as well as the usual necessities of life. (J.H.Moss/R.S.Carpenter)

88.   The identity of the 0-4-2T is now revealed as unloading of the solitary van begins. Note that the elegant gas lamp still retains its broad brim, which was added during World War II to reduce upward light emission. (J.H.Moss/R.S.Carpenter)

89.   Recorded running round on 6th September 1952 was 0-4-2T no. 5804. Similar to the 1400 class, the 5800s were not fitted for auto train working. Note the catch point, which could be held over for facing travel with the lever on the right. (H.C.Casserley)

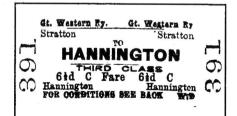

90.   Both signals are evident in this panorama from 28th February 1953, two days before the withdrawal of public passenger service, but it was the last day that such trains ran. The shed crane was rated at two tons. (Lens of Sutton)

91.   There was a choice of a seat in the sun or the shade and the fire buckets were always full of clean water. The rodding tunnel is evident; this ran to an eight-lever frame. Similar canopies can be seen in our *Branch Line to Southwold*, as both lines had Mr. Arthur Pain as the engineer for their construction. (Lens of Sutton)

→

92.   The RCTS ran a special train from Victoria on 25th April 1954 and it was hauled on the branch by 0-6-0 PT no. 1366. There was a rare appearance of a DMU on 9th April 1961 when the RCTS included the branch in a railtour from Paddington. It ran via Windsor, Malmesbury, Highworth, Faringdon and Wallingford and is shown in picture 57. (T.Wright)

→

93.   An Austin Seven from the 1930s adds to the atmosphere during another special train visit on 21st March 1962. Total closure followed on 6th August of that year. The population had risen to about 3500, an increase of 1500 in 60 years. Two signal women were recorded as employed here in 1959. The site is now occupied by dwellings. (Lens of Sutton)

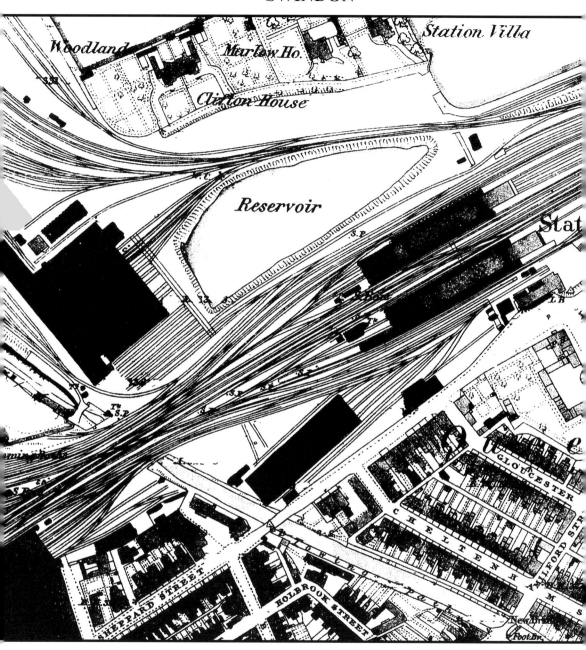

XXV. The station was not opened until 17th July 1842 and so Bristol-bound passengers passed through for the first 19 months of operation and continued their journey by road from Hay Lane, three miles to the west. A station was considered desirable here for three reasons: a branch to Gloucester was proposed, it would divide London to Bristol into three parts operationally (Reading being the other point) and the North Wilts Canal (diagonal across the lower part of this 1885 map) could bring coal to the site. Its junction with the Wilts & Berks Canal is just beyond the lower border, the coal coming along it from the Somerset pits. There were about 4000 employees here by 1875.

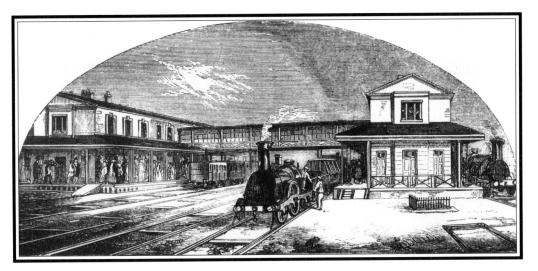

94.   An engraving from 1852 includes the building in use today on the right. The station was built at the expense of J & C Rigby in return for the right to operate the refreshment rooms on the ground floors and a hotel on the upper ones. The kitchens were in the basements. The agreement required all trains to stop here for ten minutes. The lease was sold several times and eventually bought back by the GWR in 1895 for a vast sum in order to eliminate poor food and endless problems. The premises are still known by some as "Swindlem", even though the sandwiches are now excellent. (British Railways)

XXVI. The 1925 survey at 6ins to 1 mile has the junction of the Gloucester line lower left, Highworth Junction being just beyond the right border. The goods shed and yard are parallel to the main line on the right. As a result of the presence of the GWR, the population of the town grew from 2500 in 1841 to 33,000 in 1891.

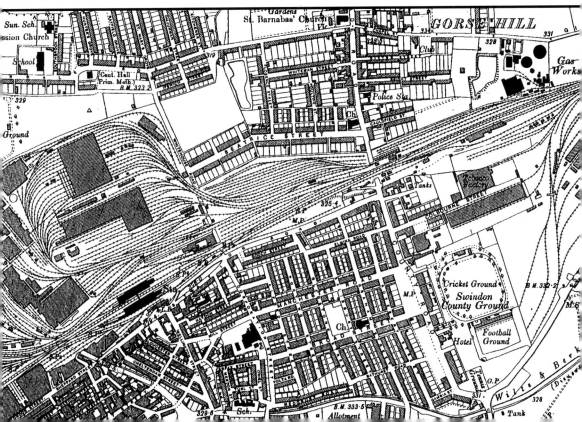

95.   An eastward view from the window on the left of the next picture includes East Box, which lasted until 13th March 1910. Its successor is shown in picture 98. On the right is "The White House", an inn that can still be seen today. (Lens of Sutton)

96.   A subway had been added in 1870 and the bay platforms were built by 1880. This panorama from the extended up platform is from 1922. Part of the massive carriage works is on the skyline. (LGRP/NRM)

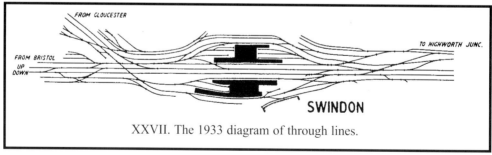

FROM GLOUCESTER

TO HIGHWORTH JUNC.

FROM BRISTOL

UP
DOWN

SWINDON

XXVII. The 1933 diagram of through lines.

97.   A lone railway observer enjoys the sight of no. 2927 *Saint Patrick* from the down main platform on 4th April 1946. One signal post is tapered wood, while the other is tubular steel. (H.C.Casserley)

98.   This panorama was recorded on 1st September 1960 from an up express, hence its lack of sharpness. On the left is the line to the through local platform (no. 1) used by Gloucester trains, next is the down main (no. 4), then the up main (no. 5) and on the right are the bays (6 and 7), followed by Cocklebury Sidings, which were added in about 1901. (M.A.N.Johnston)

——————————▶

99.   A landmark was lost on 21st October 1962 when the historic footbridge was removed by this crane. Totem signs add to the period ambience. Platform 7 was usually the starting point for trains to Highworth. (C.L.Caddy)

——————————▶

100.   The entrance building was separate and at a lower level than those seen so far; see map XXVI. Seen in the 1950s, it was demolished in about 1971 and replaced by an office tower block, a small part of which is included in picture 105. (Lens of Sutton)

101.   An illicit snap from a signal post has the down platform on the right. The three-road shed was for carriage storage and is now the site of the bay platform for Gloucester trains. To the left of it is platform 8 and to the left of its track are the two "Engine Lines", redesignated up and down through sidings in 1967. (M.J.Stretton coll.)

102.   The 19.00 Paddington to Swansea High Street is leaving platform 4 on 2nd June 1966, hauled by nos. D6891 and D6877. Platforms 3 and 2 are to the right. (J.H.Day)

103.   An up milk train was recorded a few days earlier, headed by no. D1011 *Western Thunderer*. The tanks were glass lined for easy cleaning and are seen on the up through line. East Box, seen earlier in picture 98, had 80 levers and closed on 3rd March 1968 when Swindon Panel came into use and all except platforms 5 and 8 were abandoned. (J.H.Day)

104.   No. 5 became 3 and 8 was transformed to 1. This is on the left in this view from 10th April 2002, which includes no. 43034 at the rear of the 10.59 departure to Paddington. No. 2 was created for termination of most trains from the Gloucester route. (V.Mitchell)

105.   Platform 3 is seen on the same day, as is the small section of the old down main platform that was retained for parcel and mail traffic. It opened on 8th May 1976 and has also been used for football specials. Behind it is the white top floor of Swindon Panel, which controls the lines between Challow, Bathampton, Badminton and Sapperton Tunnel. The station entrance is at the base of the 12-storey office block on the right. (V.Mitchell)

SWINDON WORKS

106.   This photograph is included to make the point that the works was a social institution, many families recording three or four generations therein. At its zenith, there were over 12,000 employees. In the few pictures that follow, we can only touch upon a subject that has justified large books exclusively and recommend a visit to the new museum on the site. (Lens of Sutton)

107.   The new "A" shop was completed in two stages, the final section being finished in 1923 and seen in 1931 when seven locomotives were being completed. They are nos. 5400, 5075, 5076, 5077, 5074, 5073 and 5419. In this decade, the peak output per annum was 149 locomotives, 470 coaches and 5340 wagons. A vast number of these items went through the repair shops. (*Steam* coll.)

108. At the west end of the site was "The Dump", officially known as "Factory Pool". On the north side of it were two tracks for cutting up locomotives. Those on the south side (right) accommodated coaches, these hiding this view from passing passengers. The photograph is from 29th October 1933. (H.C.Casserley)

109. Always forward looking, the GWR engineers embraced internal combustion, built their own road motor buses, developed the UK's first fleet of diesel railcars (see picture 51) and purchased this diesel shunting engine from John Fowler of Leeds for works use. It was photographed on 27th May 1934. (J.G.Sturt)

110. Nearing completion on 4th April 1946 was 0-6-0 PT no. 9643, every component having been made here. The Works had the dubious honour of making the last steam locomotive for BR, no. 2-10-0 *Evening Star* was named here on 18th March 1960. The premises became part of the Workshop Division of BR in 1962 and of British Rail Engineering Ltd in 1970. (H.C.Casserley)

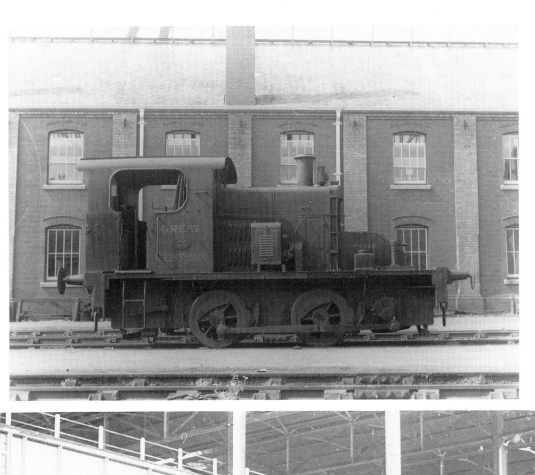

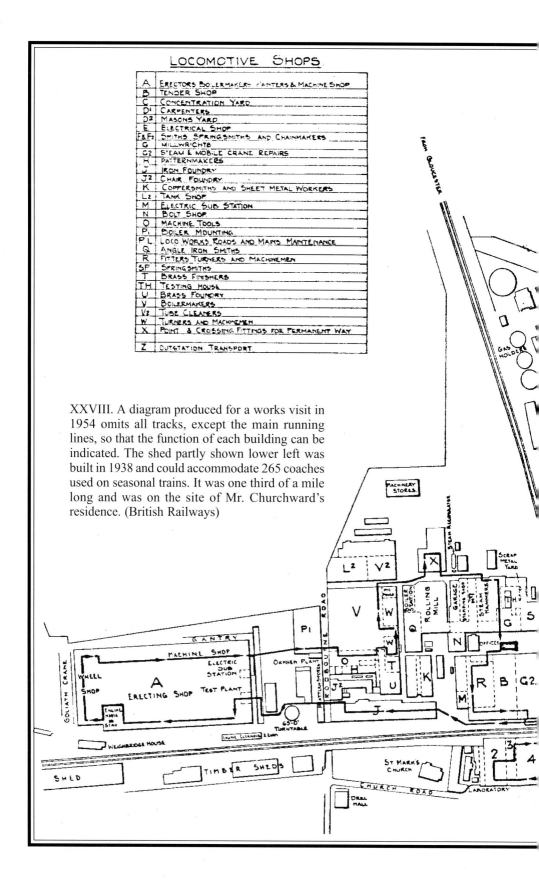

LOCOMOTIVE SHOPS

A	ERECTORS BOILERMAKERS PAINTERS & MACHINE SHOP
B	TENDER SHOP
C	CONCENTRATION YARD
D1	CARPENTERS
D2	MASONS YARD
E	ELECTRICAL SHOP
F & F2	SMITHS SPRINGSMITHS AND CHAINMAKERS
G	MILLWRIGHTS
G2	STEAM & MOBILE CRANE REPAIRS
H	PATTERNMAKERS
J	IRON FOUNDRY
J2	CHAIR FOUNDRY
K	COPPERSMITHS AND SHEET METAL WORKERS
L2	TANK SHOP
M	ELECTRIC SUB STATION
N	BOLT SHOP
O	MACHINE TOOLS
P1	BOILER MOUNTING
PL	LOCO WORKS ROADS AND MANS MAINTENANCE
Q	ANGLE IRON SMITHS
R	FITTERS TURNERS AND MACHINEMEN
SF	SPRINGSMITHS
T	BRASS FINISHERS
TH	TESTING HOUSE
U	BRASS FOUNDRY
V	BOILERMAKERS
V2	TUBE CLEANERS
W	TURNERS AND MACHINEMEN
X	POINT & CROSSING FITTINGS FOR PERMANENT WAY
Z	OUTSTATION TRANSPORT

XXVIII. A diagram produced for a works visit in 1954 omits all tracks, except the main running lines, so that the function of each building can be indicated. The shed partly shown lower left was built in 1938 and could accommodate 265 coaches used on seasonal trains. It was one third of a mile long and was on the site of Mr. Churchward's residence. (British Railways)

CARRIAGE & WAGON SHOPS

1	SAWMILL WEST END
2	SAWMILL
3	FITTING AND MACHINES
4	CARRIAGE BODY BUILDING
5	ELECTRIC TRAIN LIGHTING EQUIPMENT
7A	CARRIAGE FINISHING 7B SAWMILL
7C	POLISHING
8	CARRIAGE PAINTING
9	CARRIAGE TRIMMING
9A	LINING SEWERS (FEMALES)
10	LAUNDRY (FEMALES)
10A	POLISHING (FEMALES)
11	GENERAL LABOURERS
12A	CARPENTERS 12B SAWMILL
12C	PAINTERS 12D HAIR CARDING
13	WAGON FRAME BUILDING
13A	CARRIAGE FRAME REPAIRS
14	SMITHS
15	FITTING AND MACHINES
15A	PLUMBERS, GAS & STEAM FITTERS, TINMEN & COPPERSMITHS
16	WHEEL SHOP
16A	HEAT TREATMENT
17	ROAD VEHICLE BUILDING & REPAIRS
18	STAMPING SHOP
19A	CARRIAGE TRIMMING REPAIRS
19C	CARRIAGE LIFTING
19D	VACUUM BRAKE AND CARRIAGE BOGIE REPAIRS
20	HORSE BOX AND CARRIAGE TRUCK REPAIRS
21	WAGON BUILDING & REPAIRS WOOD SECTION, CONTAINERS
21A	WAGON REPAIRS IRON SECTION
21B	WAGON PAINTING
22	OIL AND GREASE WORKS
23	PLATELAYERS YARD MAINTENANCE & BREAKING UP YARD
24	CARRIAGE PAINT REPAIRS
24A	CARRIAGE BODY REPAIRS
24B	CARRIAGE FINISHING & SAWMILL
24C	POLISHING

111.   Thirty "Western" class diesels were built here in 1960-64, but the workforce had dwindled to about 2000 by 1973. This eastward view from 16th June 1983 includes the pattern shop of the 1873 foundry, together with no. D1015 *Western Champion* and no. D818 *Glory*. Of the "Warship" class, 38 were built here and also 56 class 14 0-6-0 diesels. The less creative task of drinking is now undertaken on the premises. (M.J.Stretton)

112.   Inside "A" shop on the same day were nos. 08795 and 08778 undergoing repair. Locomotive manufacture was resumed briefly in 1979 when 20 metre-gauge diesels were built for Kenya. Total closure of the works, which opened on 2nd January 1843, took place on 27th March 1986. (M.J.Stretton)

113.   Looking across the main line on 25th June 1986, we witness some of the last items of rolling stock to leave the site before clearance began. This is DEMU no. 205009, one of a type built at Eastleigh in the late 1950s and latterly overhauled at Swindon. (M.J.Stretton)

114.   The mighty "A" shop, seen in pictures 107 and 112 had stood in the right background of this sad panorama from February 1994. Consent for the photography had been given by Tarmac (Swindon) Ltd who were undertaking the complex redevelopment of the site. The shed in the centre of the background was the weigh house. (M.J.Stretton)

115.   As if steam could not be eliminated from the premises, a group of enterprising individuals leased 19 Shop and its overhead crane for locomotive restoration work. No. 9682, an 0-6-0 PT of the 5700 class, was undergoing surgery on 4th December 1996, while the gloves took a rest. (M.J.Stretton)

Stocklist at Steam: Museum of the
Great Western Railway in 2002.

From the National Collection -
No. 2516 Dean Goods 0-6-0
No. 4248 2-8-0T
No. 7325 2-6-0 on loan from the SVR
No. 9400 0-6-0 PT
No. 4073 *Caerphilly Castle*
No. 6000 *King George V*
Broad Gauge Replica *North Star*
GWR Diesel railcar no. 4

(top right)
116.   The GWR built barracks for its single workmen, but the building was converted to a Wesleyan Methodist Church in 1869 and to a railway museum in 1962. Its large exhibits included replica 2-2-2 *North Star*, 0-6-0 PT no. 9400, 4-4-0 no. 3717 *City of Truro*, 0-6-0 no. 2516 and 4-6-0 no. 4003 *Lode Star*. The latter is being removed on 1st March 1992; it was destined for York. The museum's closure followed in October 1999. (M.J.Stretton)

(lower right)
117.   Swindon Works experienced an unexpected return of steam era stock in 1990, due to the need to evacuate the main building of the National Railway Museum in York while roof repairs were undertaken. The collection was open to the public and ex-LSWR class T3 no. 563 of 1893 was photographed on 8th September. (P.G.Barnes)

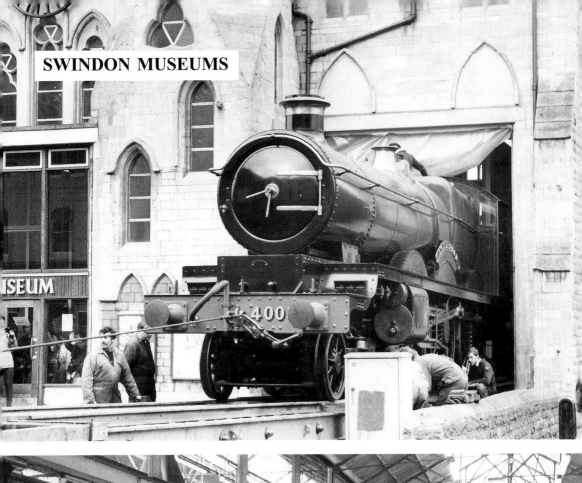

118.   Seen on the day before being presented to the public on 13th March 1997 are the private parts of deceased locomotives in the new shopping area, known bizarrely as Designer (always a person) Outlet (frequently the end of a sewer) Village (rural residences). There were other relics scattered in this former works area, which will bring a tear to many. One complete locomotive was put on show, it being 4-6-0 no. 4930 *Hagley Hall* from the Severn Valley Railway, although initially it was no. 3717 *City of Truro*. (M.J.Stretton)

XXIX. "Steam: Museum of the Great Western Railway" was the name given to Swindon Borough Council's splendid display assembled in the former machine shop. Costing an astonishing £11m, it opened on 14th June 2000 and contains many well created tableaux, some using wax figures, to portray life in the works and on the railway.

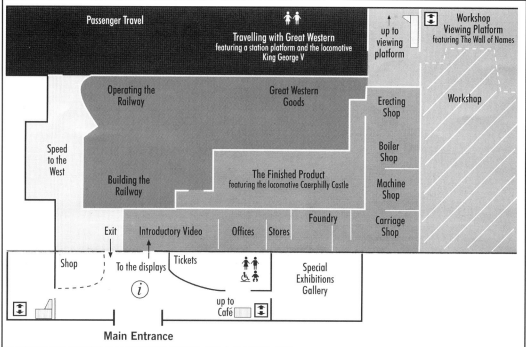

119.   The workshop can be viewed from a high level, as can passing trains. It has a comprehensive range of machine tools, but it lacks an overhead travelling crane, as seen in pictures 107 and 115. Under repair in July 2001 is 2-8-0T no. 4247. (D.Williams/*Steam*)

120.   The section titled "Travelling with Great Western" features no. 6000 *King George V*. The station includes a reconstructed booking office and a refreshment room, complete with an aged sandwich. Worshippers of the GWR should be certain to make a pilgrimage to "Steam", despite its misleading name, as it forms a worthy memorial to "God's Wonderful Railway". (*Steam*)

MP Middleton Press

Easebourne Lane, Midhurst, W Sussex. GU29 9AZ Tel: 01730 813169 Fax: 01730 812601
*If books are not available from your local transport stockist, order direct with cheque,
Visa or Mastercard, post free UK.*

BRANCH LINES
Branch Line to Allhallows
Branch Line to Alton
Branch Lines around Ascot
Branch Lines to Ashburton
Branch Lines around Bodmin
Branch Line to Bude
Branch Lines around Canterbury
Branch Lines around Chard & Yeovil
Branch Line to Cheddar
Branch Lines around Cromer
Branch Lines to East Grinstead
Branch Lines of East London
Branch Lines to Effingham Junction
Branch Lines around Exmouth
Branch Lines to Falmouth, Helston & St. Ives
Branch Line to Fairford
Branch Lines around Gosport
Branch Line to Hayling
Branch Lines to Henley, Windsor & Marlow
Branch Line to Hawkhurst
Branch Lines around Huntingdon
Branch Line to Ilfracombe
Branch Line to Kingswear
Branch Line to Lambourn
Branch Lines to Launceston & Princetown
Branch Line to Looe
Branch Line to Lyme Regis
Branch Lines around Midhurst
Branch Line to Minehead
Branch Line to Moretonhampstead
Branch Lines to Newport
Branch Lines to Newquay
Branch Lines around North Woolwich
Branch Line to Padstow
Branch Lines around Plymouth
Branch Lines to Seaton and Sidmouth
Branch Line to Selsey
Branch Lines around Sheerness
Branch Line to Shrewsbury
Branch Line to Swanage *updated*
Branch Line to Tenterden
Branch Lines around Tiverton
Branch Lines to Torrington
Branch Line to Upwell
Branch Lines of West London
Branch Lines around Weymouth
Branch Lines around Wimborne
Branch Lines around Wisbech

NARROW GAUGE
Branch Line to Lynton
Branch Lines around Portmadoc 1923-46
Branch Lines around Porthmadog 1954-94
Branch Line to Southwold
Douglas to Port Erin
Douglas to Peel
Kent Narrow Gauge
Northern France Narrow Gauge
Romneyrail
Southern France Narrow Gauge
Sussex Narrow Gauge
Two-Foot Gauge Survivors
Vivarais Narrow Gauge

SOUTH COAST RAILWAYS
Ashford to Dover
Bournemouth to Weymouth
Brighton to Worthing
Eastbourne to Hastings
Hastings to Ashford
Portsmouth to Southampton
Ryde to Ventnor
Southampton to Bournemouth

SOUTHERN MAIN LINES
Basingstoke to Salisbury
Bromley South to Rochester
Crawley to Littlehampton
Dartford to Sittingbourne
East Croydon to Three Bridges
Epsom to Horsham
Exeter to Barnstaple
Exeter to Tavistock
Faversham to Dover
London Bridge to East Croydon
Orpington to Tonbridge
Tonbridge to Hastings
Salisbury to Yeovil
Sittingbourne to Ramsgate
Swanley to Ashford
Tavistock to Plymouth
Three Bridges to Brighton
Victoria to Bromley South
Victoria to East Croydon
Waterloo to Windsor
Waterloo to Woking
Woking to Portsmouth
Woking to Southampton
Yeovil to Exeter

EASTERN MAIN LINES
Barking to Southend
Ely to Kings Lynn
Fenchurch Street to Barking
Ipswich to Saxmundham
Liverpool Street to Ilford
Saxmundham to Yarmouth

WESTERN MAIN LINES
Didcot to Swindon
Ealing to Slough
Exeter to Newton Abbot
Newton Abbot to Plymouth
Newbury to Westbury
Paddington to Ealing
Paddington to Princes Risborough
Plymouth to St. Austell
Reading to Didcot
Slough to Newbury
St. Austell to Penzance
Taunton to Exeter
Westbury to Taunton

MIDLAND MAIN LINES
St. Pancras to St. Albans

COUNTRY RAILWAY ROUTES
Andover to Southampton

Bath to Evercreech Junction
Bournemouth to Evercreech Junction
Burnham to Evercreech Junction
Cheltenham to Andover
Croydon to East Grinstead
Didcot to Winchester
East Kent Light Railway
Fareham to Salisbury
Guildford to Redhill
Reading to Basingstoke
Reading to Guildford
Redhill to Ashford
Salisbury to Westbury
Stratford upon Avon to Cheltenham
Strood to Paddock Wood
Taunton to Barnstaple
Wenford Bridge to Fowey
Westbury to Bath
Woking to Alton
Yeovil to Dorchester

GREAT RAILWAY ERAS
Ashford from Steam to Eurostar
Clapham Junction 50 years of change
Festiniog in the Fifties
Festiniog in the Sixties
Festiniog 50 years of enterprise
Isle of Wight Lines 50 years of change
Railways to Victory 1944-46
Return to Blaenau 1970-82
SECR Centenary album
Talyllyn 50 years of change
Yeovil 50 years of change

LONDON SUBURBAN RAILWAYS
Caterham and Tattenham Corner
Charing Cross to Dartford
Clapham Jn. to Beckenham Jn.
Crystal Palace (HL) & Catford Loop
East London Line
Finsbury Park to Alexandra Palace
Holbourn Viaduct to Lewisham
Kingston and Hounslow Loops
Lewisham to Dartford
Lines around Wimbledon
London Bridge to Addiscombe
Mitcham Junction Lines
North London Line
South London Line
West Croydon to Epsom
West London Line
Willesden Junction to Richmond
Wimbledon to Beckenham
Wimbledon to Epsom

STEAMING THROUGH
Steaming through Cornwall
Steaming through the Isle of Wight
Steaming through Kent
Steaming through West Hants
Steaming through West Sussex

TRAMWAY CLASSICS
Aldgate & Stepney Tramways

Barnet & Finchley Tramways
Bath Tramways
Brighton's Tramways
Bristol's Tramways
Burton & Ashby Tramways
Camberwell & W.Norwood Tramways
Clapham & Streatham Tramways
Croydon's Tramways
Dover's Tramways
East Ham & West Ham Tramways
Edgware and Willesden Tramways
Eltham & Woolwich Tramways
Embankment & Waterloo Tramways
Enfield & Wood Green Tramways
Exeter & Taunton Tramways
Greenwich & Dartford Tramways
Hammersmith & Hounslow Tramways
Hampstead & Highgate Tramways
Hastings Tramways
Holborn & Finsbury Tramways
Ilford & Barking Tramways
Kingston & Wimbledon Tramways
Lewisham & Catford Tramways
Liverpool Tramways 1. Eastern Routes
Liverpool Tramways 2. Southern Routes
Liverpool Tramways 3. Northern Routes
Maidstone & Chatham Tramways
Margate to Ramsgate
North Kent Tramways
Norwich Tramways
Reading Tramways
Seaton & Eastbourne Tramways
Shepherds Bush & Uxbridge Tramways
Southend-on-sea Tramways
Southwark & Deptford Tramways
Stamford Hill Tramways
Twickenham & Kingston Tramways
Victoria & Lambeth Tramways
Waltham Cross & Edmonton Tramways
Walthamstow & Leyton Tramways
Wandsworth & Battersea Tramways

TROLLEYBUS CLASSICS
Bournemouth Trolleybuses
Croydon Trolleybuses
Derby Trolleybuses
Hastings Trolleybuses
Maidstone Trolleybuses
Portsmouth Trolleybuses
Woolwich & Dartford Trolleybuses

WATERWAY ALBUMS
Kent and East Sussex Waterways
London to Portsmouth Waterway
West Sussex Waterways

MILITARY BOOKS
Battle over Portsmouth
Battle over Sussex 1940
Bombers over Sussex 1943-45
Bognor at War
Military Defence of West Sussex
Military Signals from the South Coast
Secret Sussex Resistance
Surrey Home Guard

OTHER RAILWAY BOOKS
Index to all Middleton Press stations
Industrial Railways of the South-East
South Eastern & Chatham Railways
London Chatham & Dover Railway
War on the Line (SR 1939-45)

BIOGRAPHY
Garraway Father & Son